AZURE DEVOPS

INTERVIEW QUESTION AND ANSWERS

Copyrights

Azure Devops Interview Question and Answers

About the Book

Azure Devops interview questions is designed to help readers learn the basic concepts of Azure Devops.

This book covers all the concepts of Azure Devops with the help of Interview question and Answers.

More than 100 Questions are included in this book which are frequently asked in current scenario.

It covers all the key areas of devops like Kanban boards , Repos , Pipelines, Artifacts, Work Items, Git , Agile, Scrum, Branching concepts, Sprints, Backlogs, Queries etc.

Contents

Copyrights 1

About the Book 2

Q 1. What is DevOps ? 7

Q2. What is Azure Devops ? 7

Q3. What is the software development cycle that Devops follows ? 7

Q4. What are benefits of Devops ? 8

Q5. What Azure DevOps Services are available ? 8

Q6. What are types of server configurations available in Devops ?............................ 8

Q7. What are types of projects in Azure Devops ? 8

Q8. What are work items in Devops ?.. 9

Q9. What work items are available in Devops ? 10

Q10. Can you enable or disbale any service in a project ? 10

Q11. What access level can be assigned to a user in project ?.................................. 10

Q12. What are Roles / (Azure Devops Groups) available for a user in project ? 10

Q13. What is kanban board ? 10

Q14. What is a work item? 11

Q15. what is a Azure Boards ? 11

Q16. What are uses of azure boards ? 11

Q17. Who works on Azure board ?... 12

Q18. What are Azure board types ? 12

Q19. What are components available in Boards ?.. 12

Q20. What is a work item ? 13

Q21. What are states in work item ?.. 14

Q22. What are the fields available in a work item ?... 14

Q23. What are the work items types available in Agile Process ? 14

Q24. What are work items available in CMMI process project ? 15

Q25. What are work items available in SCRUM process ?... 16

Q26. What are work items available in Basic process ? 16

Q27. What is a Hierarchy of work items ?... 16

Q28. Work flow of user story ?..17

Q29. What is a backlog? 17

Q30. What are types of backlog? 17

Q31. What are benefits of a backlog ? 18

Q32. How to use sprints in Azure board ?...18

Q33. What are Queries in Azure Devops Boards ? 18

Q34. What is a clause in a query ?..18

Q35. Why we a need a query?...19

Q36. What are the types of queries? 19

Q37. What are the Default queries available? 19

Q38. What is an inherited process? 19

Q39. How to create an inherited process?..19

Q40. How to customize columns in Kanban board? 19

Q41. What is a Repos?...20

Q42. What is use of Repos? 20

Q43. What is a version control? 20

Q44. What are types of versional control in Repos? 20

Q45. Difference between Git and TFVC?..20

Q46. How to clone code from Repos? 21

Q47. Can you add/ edit /delete/ rename file from azure devops server?...............................21

Q48. What are branches in Repos ? 21

Q49. Why do we need branches?...22

Q50. How does Git track current working branch?...22

Q51. What are type of branches available? 23

Q52. How can we identify any change between master and other branches? 23

Q53. What are some of git commands for branches? 23

Q54. What are pull requests in repos?..23

Q55. How to create a new pull requests? 24

Q56. What are Pipelines in Azure Devops ? 24

Q57. What is the process in pipeline?...24

Q58. What is CI and CD in Pipelines? 25

Q59. Which languages or applications can be deployed using azure pipelines? 25

Q60. Where should be your source code that needs to be deployed from azure pipelines? 25

Q61. What are Agents in Azure pipeline? 25

Q62. What are types of Agents? 26

Q63. What are approvals in azure pipeline? 26

Q64. What are Artifacts? 26

Q65. What is an Environment? 26

Q66. What is Run in Azure pipeline? 26

Q67. What is trigger in Azure pipeline? 27

Q68. What is a deployment groups in Azure pipeline? 27

Q69. What are components required in a release pipeline? 27

Q70. Explain the steps to create a release pipelne to depoy an application? 27

Q71. What is the difference between git fetch and git pull ? 28

Q72. What is Git stash ? 28

Q73. What is the difference between Git Merge and Git Rebase? 29

Q74. How to revert a commit that has already been pushed and made public? 29

Q75. What is test plan in Azure DevOps ? 30

Q76. What are the DevOps tools ? 30

Q77. At what instance can SSH be used? 30

Q78. Name some cloud platforms which can be used with Devops ? 30

Q79. What is a build process ? 30

Q80. What is Scrum ? 30

Q81. How to create a repository in Git ? 31

Q82. What is Jenkins ? 31

Q83. What is continous integration ? 31

Q84. How do you tag in a Git ? 31

Q85. How to commit code and deploy to cloud ? 31

Q86. What is continous delivery ? 31

Q87. What testing is necessary to insure a new service is ready for production? 32

Q88. What is git commit? 32

Q89. What is git push? 32

Q90. What is git checkout? 32

Q91. What is git fetch? 32

Q92. What is git add? 32

Q93. What is git merge? 32

Q94. What is git pull?..33

Q95. What is git rebase?...33

Q96. What is git clone?..33

Q97. How is DevOps different from Agile/SDLC? 33

Q98. How to view or Add team member in Devops Project ?..33

Q99. What is Monitoring ? 33

Q100. Which KPIs are used to measure of success of DevOps? 34

Q101. What do you mean by CAMS in DevOps?...34

About the Author...35

More Books by this Author...36

Q 1. What is DevOps ?

DevOps (development and operations) is an enterprise software development phrase used to mean a type of **agile relationship** between development and IT operations.

The goal of **DevOps** is to change and improve the relationship by advocating better communication and collaboration between these two business units.

Azure DevOps Server is a Microsoft product that provides

1. version control
2. reporting
3. requirements management
4. project management
5. automated builds
6. testing and
7. release management capabilities.

It covers the entire application lifecycle, and enables DevOps capabilities.

Q2. What is Azure Devops ?

Azure devops is a set of modern services which is used to

- Plan smarter (Business team)
- Collaborate better (Development team – code, build, test)
- Ship faster (operations team - deployment)

Azure devops was formerly known as **Visual Studio Team Services (VSTS)**
Azure devops is part or feature of Azure.

Q3. What is the software development cycle that Devops follows ?

Following is a Software development life cycle Devops follows : -

1. Plan   (Business team)
2. Code   (Development team)
3. Build
4. Test
5. Deploy (Operation team)
6. Operate

7. Monitor

Q4. What are benefits of Devops ?

Benefits of Devops are : -
- Fast delivery - Deploying code from Dev machine to server is very fast
- Reduce time - lot of things like (testing, deployment, rollback) are happening automatically
- Rollback - any release can be rolled back
- Quality - quality of code can be checked before deployment
- Collaboration - All teams work together to build a product
- Agility - Every commit is treated as final delivery
- Secure
- Easy to Maintain
- Easy to lean

Q5. What Azure DevOps Services are available ?

Generally there are 5 Azure Devops Servives which are available : -
1. Boards
2. Repos
3. Pipeline
4. Test Plans
5. Artifacts

Q6. What are types of server configurations available in Devops ?

There are 2 types of server configuration available : -

1. Cloud
2. On-premises

Q7. What are types of projects in Azure Devops ?

We have 2 types of projects in Azure Devops :-
1. Public projects
2. Private projects

Public projects :-
- visible to everyone
- No login is required
- unique URL
- open source project development
- unlimited number of public projects under 1 or more organizations

Private projects :-
- visible to limited users
- Must login
- unique url
- non public software development

Q8. What are work items in Devops ?

Work items are used to plan and manage your project. While creating a new project, we get an option to choose a work item. You use different types of work items to track different types of work—such as user stories or product backlog items, tasks, bugs, or issues.

Create new project   ✕

Project name *

Description

Visibility

⊕
Public

Anyone on the internet can
view the project. Certain
features like TFVC are not
supported.

🔒
Private

Only people you give
access to will be able to
view this project.

◉

∧ Advanced

Version control ⑦

Git ∨

Work item process ⑦

Basic ∨

Cancel   Create

Q9. What work items are available in Devops ?

There are mainly 4 work item process that are available : -

1. Agile
2. basic
3. CMMI
4. scrum

Q10. Can you enable or disbale any service in a project ?

Yes, we can enable/disable any service from project settings.

Q11. What access level can be assigned to a user in project ?

3 type of access level are avaiable :-
1. basic

2. stakeholder
3. visual studio subscriber

Q12. What are Roles / (Azure Devops Groups) available for a user in project ?

3 types are avaiable :-
1. Project readers
2. Project contributors
3. Project administrators

Q13. What is kanban board ?

Details of all work items to be delivered in a project.

e.g.

Q14. What is a work item?

work item is a type of work in a project like user story, bug or defect, any enhancement or refactoring in a project.

Q15. what is a Azure Boards ?

Azure board is one of the main service/ feature of Azure devops. Azure boards are compatible with scrum .

 It is used to :-

Track the work with kanban board
- pre-configured kanban board is available for visualizing our work.
- highly customizable, as as easy as drag and drop
- show live updates as changes happen

Collaborate with your team
- Work items can track anything

- Open any cards on kanban baord to add
- details
- assign the work
- @ start conversation with your team
- invite team members

Agile methodology
- backlogs -keep track of what's important
- sprints - when you team is ready to start scheduling tasks

Integrate with tools
- sync azure boards with tools team already uses like GitHub

Q16. What are uses of azure boards ?

Following are some of the uses of azure boards : -
- managing and tracking work.
- provides work done/doing by team member
- access of board can be given to stakeholder to monitor progress
- scrum, sprint can be managed
- product backlog can be maintained
- Multiple reports can be generated

Q17. Who works on Azure board ?

- whole team can work on azure board at a time like -
  dev team - tasks, stories, issues, bug etc.
- PO - manage backlog
- stakeholder - status of work, team
- scrum master - reports, progress of team

Q18. What are Azure board types ?

There are 4 type of work item process available in advanced settings while creating a new project.
- Agile
- Basic (default)

- CMMI
- Scrum

We get different type of boards based on each type

Q19. What are components available in Boards ?

There are mainly 5 components available : -
1. Work items
2. Boards
3. Backlogs
4. Sprints
5. Queries

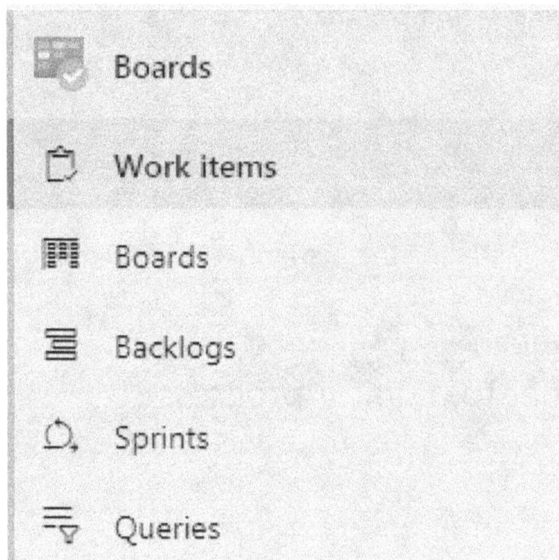

Q20. What is a work item ?

it is a unit of work. It has following characteristics
- title
- assigned to
- description
- priority

Etc.

What are types of work item available in basic Boards ?

We have following work items available while creating new work item :-
- Epic
- Issue
- Task

Epic
- It is a largest unit of work
- It can have multiple issue

issue
- It contains any bug, user story, improvements e.g login functionality
- It can can have multiple task

Task
- It is a smallest unit of work
- e.g. create table in Db, create API etc. Corresponding to login functioanlity

Q21. What are states in work item ?

It is a process of updating work item progress.
3 states are available :-
1. To Do
2. Doing
3. Done

Q22. What are the fields available in a work item ?

Following Work item fields are available

- **title** - title of the work item. 255 characters or less are allowed
- **assignedTo** - assign the work item to team member
- **state** - current state of work item like Todo, doing and done
- **reason** - represents the reason for state change. By default it is set to "Added to backlog"
- **area** - represent area path associated with a project
- **iteration** - represent the sprint or iteration in which work is to be completed
- **description** - details of work item
- **effort** - a estimate of time required to complete a work
- **discussion** - used to add a comment or any information or tag any team member
- **start date** - start date of work item
- **target date** - end date of work item

- **tag** - used to easily search a work item. Multiple tags can be added
- **priority** - four priority levels (1-4) are available
    1. resolution of work item should be addressed **as soon as possible**
    2. resolution of work item doest **not need be addressed immediatly**
    3. resolution of work item is **optional**
    4. resolution of work item is **not required**
- **attachments** - any file can be attached in a work item
- **history** - all the changes like state change are logged here

Q23. What are the work items types available in Agile Process ?

Following are the work items available : -
1. **Bug** – Missed or wrong implementation of a functionality
2. **Epic** – Represents a business requirement to be accomplished
3. **Feature** – Represents shippable component of an application
4. **Issue** – any other custom type like improvements which may not be listed
5. **Task** – smallest unit of work
6. **Test case** – tease case for feature
7. **User story** – implementation of a new work.

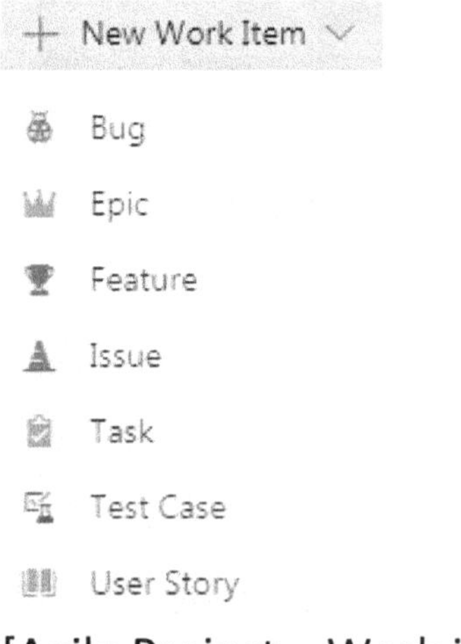

[Agile Project – Work items]

Q24. What are work items available in CMMI process project ?

CMMI – Capability Maturity model integration

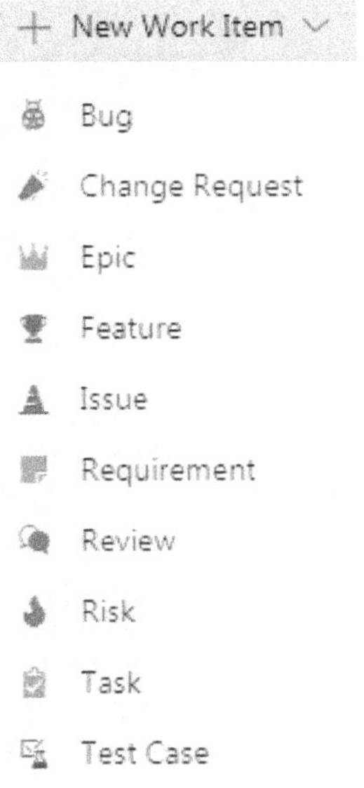

[CMMI project – Work items]

Q25. What are work items available in SCRUM process ?

1. **Bug** – Missed or wrong implementation of a functionality
2. **Epic** – Represents a business requirement to be accomplished
3. **Feature** – Represents shippable component of an application
4. **Impediment** – if your work is dependent on somebody else work
5. **Product backlog item**– work item which is tracked on board (similar to user story in agile)
6. **Task** – smallest unit of work
7. **Test case** – tease case for feature

Q26. What are work items available in Basic process ?

Following work items are available in Basic process : -

1. **Epic** – Represents a business requirement to be accomplished
2. **Issue** – any other custom type like improvements which may not be listed
3. **Task** – smallest unit of work

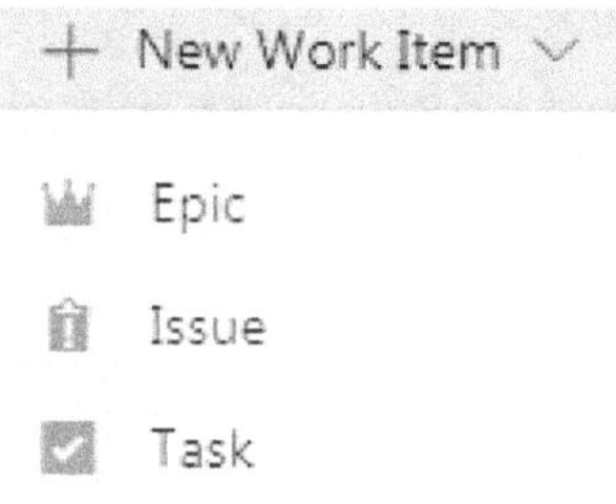

[Basic Process – Work items]

Q27. What is a Hierarchy of work items ?

- Epic is the largest unit of a work item. An epic we can have multiple feature.
- A feature can have multiple user story
- user story can have multiple Task or bug

Q28. Work flow of user story ?

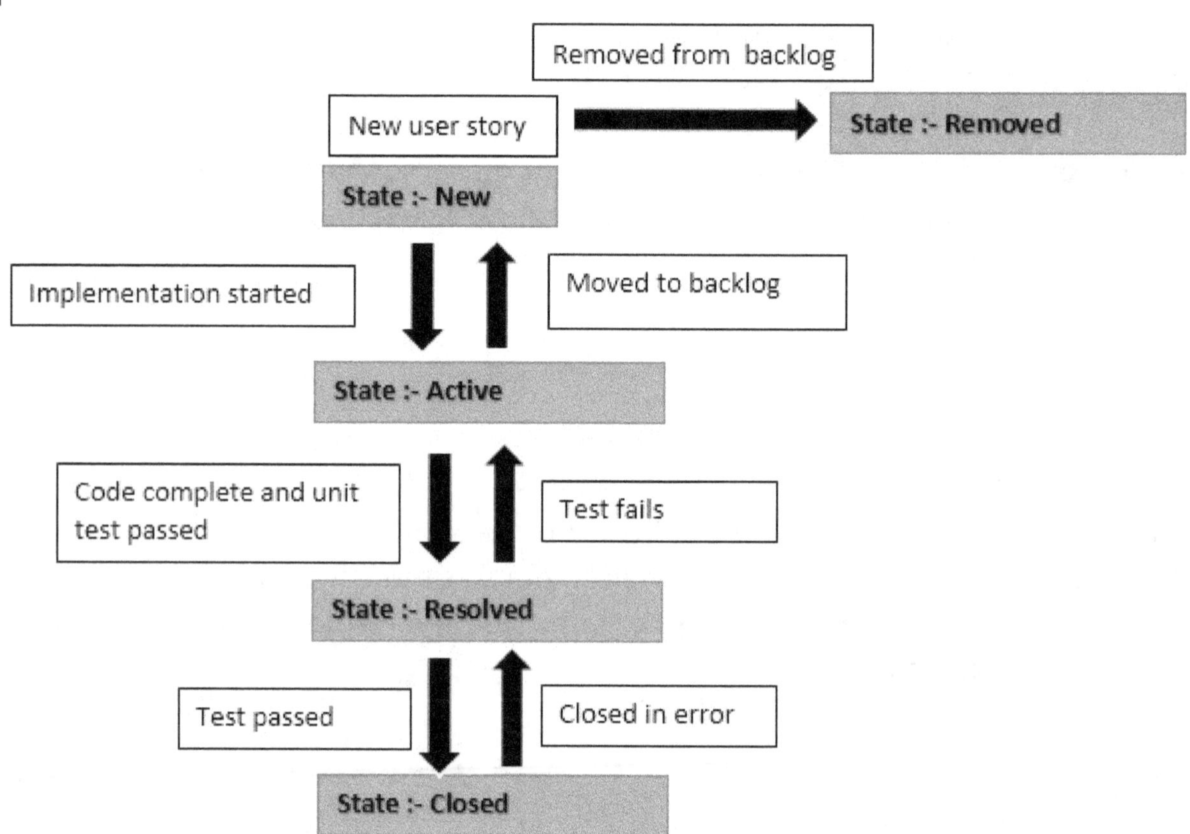

Q29. What is a backlog?

A backlog is a collection of work items which will be used in future development. In backlog we can add new work item and it also contains a planning which is a collection of sprints. We can add a new sprint in planning.

Q30. What are types of backlog?

There are 2 types of backlog : -
1. Product backlog - An ordered list of every work item needed in the product
2. Sprint backlog - Collection of work items which are in the TODO state

Q31. What are benefits of a backlog ?

- Quickly define the work item i.e. Task, issue, user story, bug, improvements etc.
- Manage priority of a work item
- Add details and estimate to the backlog items in advance
- quickly assign work items to team members
- group work items in a hierarchy
- Forecast work item for a sprint
- save time in sprint planning

Q32. How to use sprints in Azure board ?

We can create new sprint from Sprints menu option.
A new sprint is composed of : -
- Name :- Name of a sprint e.g. "sprint 1"
- Start date :- When will a sprint start
- End date :- End date of a sprint
- Location :- Project name

We can drag and drop work items from backlog and assign them to a sprint.

Q33. What are Queries in Azure Devops Boards ?

A query is a combination of logics which are applied on work items to filter out desired work item. We can create a new query by adding single clause or multiple clause.

Q34. What is a clause in a query ?

Clause is combination of logics applied to filter out a work item
It consists of –

- And/or – And/ or conditional operator
- Field – fields like work item type, assigned to, issue etc.
- Operator – operators like =, <>, contains etc.
- Value – value corresponding to selected field

Q35. Why we a need a query?

A query is used to filter work items based on several logic.
Scenario 1: all work items assigned to particular user
Scenario 2: see list of all bugs assigned

Q36. What are the types of queries?

We have 2 type of queries -
1. My queries – queries that are created by you
2. Shared queries – queries shared by another team member

Q37. What are the Default queries available?

1. Assigned to me – all work items that are assigned to you
2. Followed work items – all work items that you are following .

Q38. What is an inherited process?

We can extend any existing work process and customize it according to our needs
like we can extend the basic work process and can add more work items into
it. We cannot customize already existing processes like basic, agile, cmmi, scrum
but we can create a inherited process which is customizable work process.
Any modification in inherited process will be reflected in all projects that are
using inherited work process.

Q39. How to create an inherited process?

Go to the Organization settings > Boards > Process > (Choose a process which you want to extend). Corresponding to each pre-defined process you will get an option to "create inherited process" .

Q40. How to customize columns in Kanban board?

We can customize columns in Boards > Settings > Board > Columns

Q41. What is a Repos?

Repos stands for repository which is a container that is used to store code in a systematic way. Repo is a version control tool which is used to manage code.

Q42. What is use of Repos?

- **Storage**: - Repos is used to store code of a project
- **Tracking**: - Every change done by team can be tracked here
- **Synchronization**: - Mutiple team members can work on same code at a time that can be synced or merged easily
- **Branches**: - Mutiple branches can be created from one project for different tasks or environments. Like for "Development" environment, we can have one branch and for "QA" environment we can have another branch referring to same project
- **Tags**: - using tags feature we can avoid creating multiple versions for the same build.

Q43. What is a version control?

- Version control is a system which is used to track and manage each and every change in a code done by an individual or any team member
- Using this we can track every change done by a team member

Q44. What are types of versional control in Repos?

2 types of version control are available in Repos: -
- Git: - Distributed version control

- TFVC (Team foundation version control): - Centralized version control

Q45. Difference between Git and TFVC?

Git	TFVC
Distributed version control	Centralized version control
Local repo is available I.e., Replica of main repository is cloned to Local repo	Local repo is not available Developers directly works on main repository since local repo is not available
Developers can push all the changes from their local repo to main repository	There may be an issue when multiple developers are working on same file and pushing it to a repository
Operations are fast as everything happens on local repo e.g., switching of branches is fast since it is happening in local repo	Bit slower compared to Git since operations are happening on centralized repo e.g., switching of branches take bit time as code will be travelling from server to a local machine

Q46. How to clone code from Repos?

We can clone code from Repos in multiple ways

- **Using Git command**: - you can use "git clone <path of repository>" command to clone repos into your local folder
- **Using Visual studio**: - from visual studio you can go to "team explorer > local git repositories" and enter the path of your Repos
- **Tortoise Git**: - using tortoise git > git clone option you can clone main repository to your local system

Q47. Can you add/edit/delete/rename file from devops server?

Yes, we can add file or folder in devops server.

- **Add new file/folder**: -Click on the 3 (…) dots corresponding to a project name, from there we will get an option to add new file or folder
- **Edit**: - Open the file that you want to modify and go to the "Contents" tab. In that tab we can click an "Edit" button to modify the file.

- **Delete**: - Open the file that you want to delete. In the "Contents" tab open the 3 (...) dots menu button. In that we have an option to "Delete" a file
- **Rename**: - Open the file that you want to rename. In the "Contents" tab open the 3 (...) dots menu button. In that we have an option to "Rename" a file.

Q48. What are branches in Repos ?

By default, we have a **"master"** branch which contains all the files of a repository. But if we do not want to commit a code in our main master branch then we can create a **separate branch** from our main master branch. Creating a new branch do not copy files from main master branch, it will just **create a new pointer snapshot** which will point to new branch. So, creating multiple branches will not take any more space. It is just pointing to new branch without replicating files from main master branch.

For e.g., we have main master branch that contains all our files. From this master branch we can further create "Dev" branch for development environment and "QA" branch for QA environment.

Later, we can merge all the changes of multiple branches into master branch.

Q49. Why do we need branches?

Our main "master" branch is a production ready branch I.e., if we need to release our software/project then the "master" branch is our PROD ready branch. To avoid corrupting our main master branch we generally create new branches for development purposes and once all the changes are verified in QA then we can merge our changes in master branch. In summary: -

- Use branch to avoid any break in master branch
- To develop a new functionality
- To work in different environments like dev, qa etc.
- To create a POC
- To do any kind of R & D.

Q50. How does Git track current working branch?

Git tracks current working branch with the help of **HEAD**. Suppose we
have switched our branch from master branch to QA branch then the HEAD will
point to QA branch.
We can use CLI command to know about current branch
[git branch]
This command will print all branches that are available in our Repos and our
current branch will be marked with * (Asterix) symbol
e.g., * master
So, like master is our current branch
We can switch between branches using git command: -
[get checkout <branch name>]

Q51. What are type of branches available?

We have 2 type of branches : -
- Local branch
- Server branch

From visual studio we can access both type of branches.
- Visual studio > team explorer > remotes/origin - server branch
- Visual studio > team explorer > master - local branch

Q52. How can we identify any change between master and other branches?

In azure devops > branches we can track any difference of code between master
and another branch with the help of **[Behind | Ahead] column**
For e.g., if we have a "Dev" branch and in this branch, we have 2| 1 set in [Behind
| Ahead] column
 than that means "Dev" branch is 2 commits behind of master branch and 1
commit ahead. By clicking on these values, we can also track and compare these
changes with master branch.

Q53. What are some of git commands for branches?
- Create new branch: -
  - [git branch <new branch name>]

- Check list of branches: -
    - [git branch]
    Note: - it will print list of branches with default branch decorated with * (Asterix) symbol
- Switch branch: -
    - [git checkout <branch name>]

Q54. What are pull requests in repos?

Pull requests **combine the merge and review of your code** into a single collaborative process.

Benefits of pull requests: -

- Merge your code into the master branch
- Reviewers can review it before approving the merge
- Reviewers can leave comments, approve or reject the code
- Team can give feedback on changes in branches

Q55. How to create a new pull requests?

Here are the steps to create new pull requests

1. Go to Repos > Pull requests
2. **Select Branch to merge**: - select your source and destination branches e.g., "select source branch" into "master branch"
3. **Title**: - input any relative title
4. **Description**: - Write a meaningful description about a merge
5. **Reviewers**: - Select single or multiple reviewers to review your code
6. **Work items to link**: - Select any work item related to your commit
7. **Tags**: - write any related tags
8. **create/ create as draft**: - press the create button to create a pull request or you can choose "create as draft" to commit it later.

Q56. What are Pipelines in Azure Devops ?

- Pipeline in devops is a set of process (automated or manually triggered) which is used to move your project code to users.
- It is a process to deploy your code from particular location to servers. From there end users can have access to application
- Pipelines will also build and test your code.

Q57. What is the process in pipeline?

- **Repos**: - Get the code from Repos which you want to deploy
- **Build**: - Build the code so that any error can be found before deployment
- **Test**: - Unit testing of code to avoid any bugs or issues
- **Deploy**: - Move the code to servers .

Q58. What is CI and CD in Pipelines?

CI (Continuous integration): - CI is used to *automate tests and build process* of your projects. Bugs or any build issue can be detected in CI process. It is also known as *Build pipeline*.

CD (Continuous delivery): - CD is used to *automate deploy and test process* of your projects. It is performed in multiple stages for different environments like Production, QA, Staging, Development etc. To ensure the quality of a project. It is also known as *Release pipeline*.

CI and CD can be either triggered manually or automatically at each commit, at particular time or at fix interval etc.

Q59. Which languages or applications can be deployed using azure pipelines?

Azure pipelines are framework or language independent.
We can deploy any application or frameworks or language using pipelines.
e.g., .NET, .NET Core, C++, Angular, Python, Ruby, Java, JavaScript etc.

Q60. Where should be your source code that needs to be deployed from azure pipelines?

Code should be in any version control system like: -

- Azure Repos Git
- Bitbucket Cloud
- GitHub
- GitHub Enterprise Server
- Other Git

- Subversion

Q61. What are Agents in Azure pipeline?

To build or deploy an application on Azure pipeline, we need at least one agent. An agent is a installable software which runs a job. A System always begin one job when you build or deploy an application.

Q62. What are types of Agents?

We have 2 types of Agents in azure pipeline: -
1. **Microsoft-hosted Agent**: - Agent by default provided by Microsoft. It performs tasks like getting code from repos, build it, prepare VM etc.
2. **Self-hosted Agent**: - Installed by user to have more control over Agent.

Q63. What are approvals in azure pipeline?

Approvals are set of validations which are required before a deployment. Like before deploying a code to "Production" environment we would need a permission from someone in a team.

Q64. What are Artifacts?

An Artifact is a collection of files or packages which we get after publishing an application. These artifacts are required for a deployment. These are the required files to run an application.
These artifacts are created from build pipeline and are made available to release pipeline.

Q65. What is an Environment?

An environment is a place or server where we deploy our application.
Environment can be: -
- Development [DEV]
- QA
- Staging
- Production [PROD]
An environment is a collection of resources like VMs, web apps, containers etc.

A release pipeline can deploy a code to multiple Environments at a time.

Q66. What is Run in Azure pipeline?

An execution of build or release pipeline is known as Run.

Q67. What is trigger in Azure pipeline?

A trigger is a setup which tells when to execute a pipeline. It can be configured according to new push in repo, at particular scheduled time or upon completion of any other build etc.
Like we have these triggers available: -

- **Continuous deployment trigger** : Enabling this trigger will create a new release every time a new build is available.
- **Pull request trigger** : Enabling this will create a release every time a selected artifact is available as part of a pull request workflow.

Q68. What is a deployment groups in Azure pipeline?

Deployment groups is a link between Azure devops and virtual machines (VMs) I.e., it connects your Azure devops with virtual machines.

Q69. What are components required in a release pipeline?

To create a new pipeline, we need to add: -

1. **Artifact**: - We need to choose a Source for an Artifact. Following are some of the source types available in azure devops : -
    - Build
    - Azure repository
    - GitHub
    - Azure Artifacts
    - Docker hub etc.
2. **Stage**: - A stage refers to a particular environment where we want to deploy our code. Some examples of Stage are: - Development, QA, Staging, Production etc.
3. **Deployment Server**: - You need to choose a deployment server in Stage. There are many templates available by default. E.g., for .NET application we can choose "IIS Website deployment" template.

Steps to deploy an application using release pipeline: -

1. **Create a Virtual machine (VM)**: - you need to create a VM using cloud tools like Azure, AWS etc. This VM will act as a server where you can host your application.

2. **Deployment Groups**: - Create a new deployment group and link your VM with it. Deployment Groups will provide you a script which you can execute in a power shell of your VM.

3. **Releases > Artifacts**: - Add an Artifacts which you want to release. Artifacts is s set of build files which you want to deploy on server.

4. **Releases > Stages**: - Select a template where you want to deploy your application. Like most common one Is "IIS website deployment"

5. **Release > tasks**: - Select a deployment group where you want to deploy your application. This is mandatory. Without it, we cannot proceed further

6. **Save and create release**: - After doing all configuration press the "save" option and after that press "create release" button.

Git Fetch	Git Pull
Does not integrate any new data into your working files	Does not integrate any new data into your working files
Git fetch only downloads new data from a remote repository	Git pull updates the current HEAD branch with the latest changes from the remote server
Users can run a Git fetch at any time to update the remote-tracking branches	Tries to merge remote changes with your local ones
Command - git fetch origin	Command - git pull origin master

A developer working with a current branch wants to switch to another branch to work on something else, but the developer doesn't want to commit changes to your unfinished work. The solution to this issue is Git stash. Git stash takes your modified tracked files and saves them on a stack of unfinished changes that you can reapply at any time.

Q73. What is the difference between Git Merge and Git Rebase?

Suppose you are working on a new feature in a dedicated branch, and another team member updates the master branch with new commits. You can use these two functions:

Git Merge

To incorporate the new commits into your feature branch, use Git merge.

- Creates an extra merge commit every time you need to incorporate changes

- But, it pollutes your feature branch history

Git Rebase

As an alternative to merging, you can rebase the feature branch on to master.

- Incorporates all the new commits in the master branch

- It creates new commits for every commit in the original branch and rewrites project history

Q74. How to revert a commit that has already been pushed and made public?

There are two ways that you can revert a commit:

Remove or fix the bad file in a new commit and push it to the remote repository. Then commit it to the remote repository using:

git commit –m "commit message"

Create a new commit that undoes all the changes that were made in the bad commit. Use the following command:

git revert <commit id>

Example: git revert 34egh68k

Q75. What is test plan in Azure DevOps ?

Azure DevOps Test Plan provides all the tools you need to successfully test your applications. Create and run manual test plans, generate automated tests and collect feedback from users.

Q76. What are the DevOps tools ?

The DevOps tools are used in the DevOps process and usually includes various categories like

- Versioning – Git
- DevOps Automation – Jenkins, Puppet, Ansible
- Test Automation – Selenium, Jmeter
- Virtualization – Docker, Kubernetes
- Build tool - Gradle

Q77. At what instance can SSH be used?

SSH can be used to : -

- log into a remote machine and work on the command line.
- Tunnel into the system to facilitate secure encrypted communications between two untrusted hosts over an insecure network.

Q78. Name some cloud platforms which can be used with Devops ?

Popular Cloud computing platform used for DevOps implementation are:

- Google Cloud
- Amazon Web Services
- Microsoft Azure

Q79. What is a build process ?

A build is a method in which the source code is put together to check whether it works as a single unit. In the build creation process, the source code will undergo compilation, inspection, testing, and deployment.

Q80. What is Scrum ?

Scrum is basically used to divide your complex software and product development task into smaller chunks, using iterations and incremental practises. Each iteration is of two weeks. Scrum consists of three roles: Product owner, scrum master and Team.

Q81. How to create a repository in Git ?

To create a repository, you must create a directory for the project if it does not exist, then run command "git init". By running this command .git directory will be created inside the project directory.

Q82. What is Jenkins ?

Jenkins is an open source continuous integration tool which is written in Java language. It keeps a track on version control system and to initiate and monitor a build system if any changes occur. It monitors the whole process and provides reports and notifications to alert the concern team.

Q83. What is continous integration ?

When multiple developers or teams are working on different segments of same web application, we need to perform integration test by integrating all the modules. To do that an automated process for each piece of code is performed on daily bases so that all your code gets tested. And this whole process is termed as continuous integration.

Q84. How do you tag in a Git ?

We have following command to create tags in git
Git tag v0.1

Q85. How to commit code and deploy to cloud ?

- Create a deployment environment
- Get a Latest code
- Create your pipeline
- Activate your pipeline
- Commit a change and update the App.

Q86. What is continous delivery ?

Continuous Delivery means an extension of Constant Integration which primarily serves to make the features which some developers continue developing out on some end users because soon as possible. During this process, it passes through several stages of QA, Staging etc., and before for delivery to the PRODUCTION system.

Q87. What testing is necessary to insure a new service is ready for production?

Continuous testing

Q88. What is git commit?

Commits the changes to the HEAD (staging area)

Q89. What is git push?

Sends the changes to the remote repository

Q90. What is git checkout?

Switch branch or restore working files

Q91. What is git fetch?

Fetch the latest history from the remote server and updates the local repo.

Q92. What is git add?

adds the file changes to the staging area

Q93. What is git merge?

Joins two or more branches together

Q94. What is git pull?

Fetch from and integrate with another repository or a local branch (git fetch + git merge)

Q95. What is git rebase?

Process of moving or combining a sequence of commits to a new base commit

Q96. What is git clone?

clones the git repository and creates a working copy in the local machine

Q97. How is DevOps different from Agile/SDLC?

Agile software development methodology focuses on the development of software.

DevOps on the other hand is responsible for development as well as deployment of the software in the safest and most reliable way possible.

Q98. How to view or Add team member in Devops Project ?

You can view or add a team member in project Settings.

Go to project settings>Teams.

Here you can add or view team member.

Q99. What is Monitoring ?

Monitoring provides feedback from production. It delivers information about an application's performance, downtime, uptime, response time etc.

Q100. Which KPIs are used to measure of success of DevOps?

The full form of KPIs is **Key Parameter Indicators**. Some of the most popular KPIs to indicate the measure the success of DevOps is as follows:

- The pass percentage of the automated tests
- Error rate
- Frequency of deployment
- Deployment time
- Change volume
- Availability
- Application performance
- Application usage

Q101. What do you mean by CAMS in DevOps?

CAMS is an acronym in DevOps, which stands for

- **C**ulture
- **A**utomation
- **M**easurement
- **S**haring

It is used to describe the basic needs of DevOps technology.

About the Author

Vishal garg

Vishal Garg is a technical writer with a passion for writing technical books. He has passion for learning new technologies and share the knowledge with everyone. He is well versed in technologies like Azure, Devops, Angular, .Net core, C# etc. He also shares his knowledge with the community through book writings, blog writings , presentations etc.
He has written books on different technologies as well and got a positive reviews on that. He followed a very unique way to cover all major concepts.

With the help of various surveys and real time experience a question bank of a particular topic are compiled and logged in a book.

He is hoping that all readers will be benefited from this book and looking forward to put in more effort to produce quality books in future.

Note : If you like the book, please take some time to put in positive reviews on Amzon website. This feedback will encourage him to produce more quality books in future.

More Books by this Author

- .Net Core Simplified: Interview QA

- Angular Simplified: Learning made easy

- C# Interview Question and Answers: Simplified